The Gardener's Year

TIPS AND TRICKS TO KEEP YOUR GARDEN GREEN THROUGH THE SEASONS

PIPPA GREENWOOD

summersdale

THE GARDENER'S YEAR

An Hachette UK Company
www.hachette.co.uk

Summersdale Publishers Ltd
Part of Octopus Publishing Group Limited
Carmelite House
50 Victoria Embankment
LONDON
EC4Y 0DZ
UK

www.summersdale.com

Printed and bound in the Czech Republic

ISBN: 978-1-78685-765-1

Substantial discounts on bulk quantities of Summersdale books
are available to corporations, professional associations and other
organisations. For details contact general enquiries: telephone:
+44 (0) 1243 771107 or email: enquiries@summersdale.com.

Note from the Author

We all need a nudge every now and then, a little prompt to ensure that things get done when they should, and gardeners and aspiring gardeners are no exception! So it seemed like a good idea to create a book to make it easier to get your gardening life in order – quickly and simply, without the need to wade through pages and pages of text. After all, if you have an hour or two to spend in your garden, surely it is important that as much of that time as possible is spent in the garden gardening, not reading up about what to do! So, if you're after a gentle reminder just open the book and then out you go to get on with some *gardening* – take the book and a favourite pencil with you and you can also add your own notes and comments in the appropriate month.

January

Early January

ORNAMENTALS

If ponds freeze over, avoid smashing the ice as this may cause wildlife or fish to be injured; instead, hold the base of a saucepan of boiling water on the surface and allow it to melt a hole in the ice. Potentially toxic gasses will escape through the hole, meaning wildlife and fish should remain unharmed.

Check that tree stakes and ties, and any ties keeping climbers in position, are in good condition and replace them if necessary. Windy weather is likely, so they need to perform well, but make sure that they are not too tight or chafing and adjust to fit.

Place new mulch around the base of hellebores, or top up existing ones – choose 'clean' mulch such as chipped bark, as this will reduce the splash-back effect on to the flowers as they open.

Use hessian or bubble wrap to insulate the outer surface of containers – the worst of the weather is generally yet to come and well-wrapped roots are essential if plants in pots are to survive the winter in style. Alternatively, plunge the entire pot into a spare bit of soil, making sure that you don't bury it too deeply.

Sow some sweet peas, choosing any variety with a good strong perfume. Sown in pots of good quality multi-purpose compost now – with or without any additional heat – they should germinate and provide strong plants for later in the year.

Give yourself a treat when the weather outside is really grim and peruse the seed catalogues to check out new vegetable varieties. Making a note of any varieties that show good disease resistance is also worthwhile… then start drawing up your order!

Make sure you've completed your order for seed potatoes. The best selection is generally available by mail order/online, but it is also worth looking to see what is available from your local garden centre. If space is limited, choose early varieties as these take up the least room and spend the shortest amount of time in the ground, so making way for a different crop later in the year.

Fruit trees, bushes and canes will all benefit from a feed of sulphate of potash, or rock potash, as this helps to keep them flowering and fruiting later in the year. Use about 15–30 g per square metre, applying the potash over the entire root area, raking in lightly if possible, watering well and then topping off with mulch, such as well-rotted manure or garden compost.

As long as the soil is not frozen solid or excessively wet, this is a good time to buy and plant bare-root fruit plants. The best selection is usually available from specialist nurseries, and the varieties on offer locally are often those best suited to the local conditions.

This is the final call to clean out the greenhouse and cold frame, if you've put it off up until now. Scrubbing down surfaces with a stiff brush and some soapy water will help to reduce the risk of problems occurring with new plants early in the year – it will lower numbers of any overwintering pests and diseases and allow more light through to the plants.

Don't forget to provide a regular supply of food for birds – they're a delight to have in the garden and for much of the year many of them help to keep pest numbers down. You can buy a great selection of bird foods, but do save scraps such as unsalted nuts, cooked rice and pasta, fruit and cheese and biscuits too, but avoid anything that is spicy or salty.

A source of fresh, clean (and unfrozen!) water is essential for birds to drink and bathe in. Replace water regularly, cleaning out the container each time, and make sure that supplies of both water and food are positioned in a spot well out of the way of predators like cats – on a bird table or the top of a hedge, perhaps.

Check that any outdoor taps and pipes are properly insulated, so that they are not damaged during freezing conditions. I find that bubble wrap, held in place with twine, works brilliantly. In extreme conditions it is worth turning the water supply to outdoor taps off at the mains, just in case!

Collect or rake up fallen leaves and twigs that have landed or redistributed themselves around the garden – much of this material makes great compost, and by removing it you reduce the risk of moisture accumulating around the plants and causing them to deteriorate.

Late January

ORNAMENTALS

Sow some summer bedding plants. To ensure that they're as big and beautiful as possible in the coming summer, seeds of flowers such as pelargoniums, gazanias and lobelias need to be sown now, in good quality compost in a heated propagator.

Winter bedding plants like pansies can get badly battered by extreme weather and the discoloured flowers may then succumb to grey mould. Keep the plants looking good and healthy by regularly removing faded or badly battered flowers, and any foliage showing signs of grey, fuzzy fungal growth.

Visit a good garden centre or peruse the catalogues for some summer-flowering bulbs. These should be in stock now and will help to bring stunning colour to beds, borders and containers for years to come. There are some wonderful types available, including lilies, alliums, crinums, dahlias, *Tigridia* and *Ornithogalum*; great for planting in suitable conditions between now and March – just make sure the soil is not very wet or frozen solid.

Flowers on shrubs such as magnolias can be badly damaged by severe frosts, even when in bud, putting paid to their annual display. Keep them snug and protected by wrapping the top-growth in a couple of layers of horticultural fleece, tying or pinning it firmly in place.

Early flowering bulbs will be up and blooming soon, so make sure that as their foliage starts to appear they're not swamped by weeds, fallen leaves or other debris.

As soon as you get your seed potatoes, start to chit them – this enables them to produce short, sturdy shoots. Place the tubers 'rose' (or plumpest end) uppermost in old egg cartons or seed trays in a cool but frost-free spot with plenty of natural light. Don't forget to label each tray… seed potatoes can look very similar!

If the soil is not wet or frozen solid it's worth forking in some well-rotted manure or garden compost to improve its fertility and texture, ready for the growing year ahead. Getting the soil prepared now will save you time feeding and watering later in the year and is often key to getting a good crop from your veg, fruit and herb plants.

Make first sowings of crops such as cauliflower, radish, mooli and lettuce. Sown in a greenhouse or on a windowsill, now, the seed will germinate rapidly. If you sow seeds in individual 'cells' it makes for much easier transplanting later on. As each of the seedlings or small plants will have its own undisturbed rootball, they should transplant with less disturbance and grow away without a check in growth.

If you didn't get around to pruning your summer-fruiting raspberries last year then you can just get away with it now – cut the canes that fruited last year back to a few centimetres above ground level and then tie in all of last year's new canes.

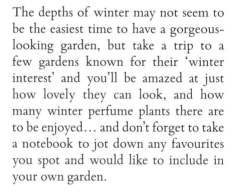

The depths of winter may not seem to be the easiest time to have a gorgeous-looking garden, but take a trip to a few gardens known for their 'winter interest' and you'll be amazed at just how lovely they can look, and how many winter perfume plants there are to be enjoyed… and don't forget to take a notebook to jot down any favourites you spot and would like to include in your own garden.

Frosted grass is very easily damaged, so wherever possible try to avoid walking on lawns, grass paths or other grassed areas when they are frosted or snow-covered. By keeping the blades of grass intact now you'll save yourself time and energy later in the year.

January is a brilliant month for planning – take a long hard look at basic garden features like the lawn and flower and veg beds, and consider whether they are the size and shape you need. For instance, do you perhaps want less lawn and more veg plot? Is it time to install the pond or water feature that you've always dreamed about?

Prune any remaining apples and pears that you did not sort out earlier in the winter. Remember to ensure that you remove any areas showing canker infection (see below), and any dead, damaged or dying stems too.

This is the best time of year to spot, and sort out, infections that develop on the stems or trunks of deciduous trees and shrubs – bare stems are easy to inspect and simpler to prune! Elliptical, slightly flaky and often somewhat sunken patches on the bark of apple and pear trees are probably due to apple canker infection, which, if left on the plant, can spread and ring entire stems or even trunks. Use a sharp pair of secateurs or a pruning saw to remove the entire cankered area or stem. Bin or burn the cankered parts as the fungus can easily spread to other parts of the tree.

Look out for overwintering lacewings and ladybirds. These great garden allies are often found tucked away in unexpected places: in the garden, in sheds, in garages and even in your house. However house-proud you are, please leave them be as they need all the help they can get, and are such wonderful predators of pests such as greenfly and blackfly. I often find ladybirds in vast quantities within the window frames of a south-facing bay window!

Anything which has been planted within the last few months will be potentially prone to winter damage, even if it's a plant that is basically perfectly hardy, so use well-pegged-down fleece or 'cages' made from chicken wire, packed full of dry leaves or straw, to protect them in their first winter. It is essential that air circulation is still good, or else there are more likely to be problems with grey mould (*Botrytis*) and other fungal infections.

Winter wet is even more likely to seriously damage or even kill plants than winter cold. Plants in containers will need to be watered, but keep this to a minimum and make sure that all winter planters and containers are raised off the ground, so that drainage is not impeded. For this you can buy smart plant pot 'feet' or, for larger containers, tuck a few half bricks beneath the lower rim of the container and they'll do the job well, not cost a penny, and be out of sight too! It is also worth checking that guttering on the house or garage is kept clear, so that water does not drain onto plants beneath.

Notes

February

Early February

ORNAMENTALS

Avoid stepping or standing on flower beds if they are covered with frost or snow or are waterlogged. Wet soil is really easily compacted, which can badly damage its structure. If you need to do extensive work that involves standing on the soil, lay boards on the surface to minimise damage.

If the soil is not too wet, then this is a great time to dig or fork over any areas that you would like to plant up or alter extensively in the coming months. On a heavy clay soil I always use a fork (rather than a spade) as this is less likely to compact the soil. Incorporating plenty of well-rotted manure or garden compost as you go will also help to improve soil texture.

Continue to regularly deadhead any winter-flowering bedding plants such as pansies and pompom daisies; this helps to keep them flowering and also reduces the risk of weather-battered petals becoming a source of grey mould – a nasty infection which can cause extensive dieback.

Sow seeds of pelargoniums, gazanias, snapdragons and other slower-growing bedding plants. You will need a heated propagator for this and somewhere well lit and warm to grow the plants on.

Once sweet-pea seedlings are 8–10 cm tall, pinch out the tips of each using either sharp scissors or a thumbnail. This will help to encourage the young plants to develop side shoots, making for more flowers later in the year.

Many vegetable seeds can be sown outside later this month, or early next, so make sure you get your preparation started. After clearing the area of weeds, debris and stones, fork it over, incorporate well-rotted manure or garden compost and then cover the areas where you're intending to sow the seeds (a covering of a couple of layers of fleece or polythene, or a cloche, will allow the soil to warm up slightly and keep off excess rain, so improving sowing conditions for when the time arrives).

Continue to sow seeds of favourite varieties of greenhouse crops such as chilli peppers, sweet peppers, aubergines and tomatoes. Seeds sown in a heated propagator will germinate promptly and, provided you have a warm, well-lit spot, the resulting seedlings (and later young plants) should grow away well.

This really is the last call for winter pruning of fruit trees – left any later and the trees may be moving into growth, especially in warmer or more sheltered gardens. And don't forget to take the secateurs to autumn-fruiting raspberries too. Prune all the canes back to a couple of centimetres above soil level, and then apply good, bulky organic mulch around the plants, taking care to keep the mulch just clear of the canes. The raspberries will soon start to produce new canes which will then bear fruit in late summer and into autumn.

Paths, patios, driveways and steps can become very dangerous when covered with ice, but if you use salt on these areas you'll need to ensure that nearby flower beds, hedges or large plants are not contaminated by salt run-off or leaching. Use a pressure washer or stiff yard broom and soapy water to scrub off algal deposits, to make the surface less hazardous.

Continue to keep garden birds well supplied with food and fresh water and then install a few bird boxes too. It may be too early for nesting to start but, installed now, boxes are more likely to be used a little later in the year, and in the meantime may be used as roosting places that provide some protection from bitter cold. Choose well-constructed boxes, ideally with the RSPB or BTO seal of approval, and position them well out of the way of cats and other predators, in a sheltered spot, ideally facing north-east (this means they will be less likely to get too hot later in the year).

If you have not already given your hedges a good trim, make sure you tackle deciduous hedges now before there is any chance of birds starting to nest in them.

Late February

ORNAMENTALS

As soon as winter-flowering heathers have finished flowering, give them a light trim using secateurs, or shears on larger clumps. Cut so that you remove the faded flower stem and just a little bit of stem below. Trimming at this time of year will help to keep the plants growing good and dense and will also encourage better flowering next year.

Lift and divide long-established clumps of snowdrops and also winter-flowering aconites. After a few years the clumps become quite congested and so flowering will be less reliable. Unlike many other garden bulbs, both of these winter charmers will respond well to being lifted, divided and replanted while 'in the green' or bearing green foliage. Make sure you fork in leaf mould or garden compost before replanting, and that the bulbs are planted as deep as they were before you dug them out.

Think ahead to the summer and buy yourself some summer-flowering bulbs. Many do just as well in tubs and planters as they do garden borders, so use them wherever you can. Some of my favourites include lilies, *Allium*, *Tigridia pavona*, *Galtonia candicans*, *Crinum* spp. and *Ornithogalum*. Make sure that the soil is well drained – if necessary, fork in some horticultural grit before planting.

There is still a lot of vegetable and herb seed-sowing to do over the coming weeks, so buy in a stock of good-quality seeds and cuttings or multi-purpose compost for seed-sowing. Freezing-cold compost is not going to speed up germination of seeds, so put at least one bag in your greenhouse or porch to warm it up slightly before you use it.

If you have a plentiful supply of strawberry plants then why not force a few? By covering the plants with a couple of layers of fleece, a cloche or a pull-out fleece-covered tunnel cloche you will be able to bring the plants in to cropping just a little earlier than the rest… mmm!

This is a great time to plant bare-root raspberry canes – the best range is generally available from specialist nurseries and mail-order/online suppliers. If planting on a heavy soil, it helps to position the canes on a slight ridge to reduce the risk of winter wetness. Each cane needs to be planted about 45 cm apart, and the summer varieties in particular will require a support system – ideally sturdy posts with a system of galvanised straining wires.

Make sure that all seedling vegetable plants have plenty of natural light, or else they are likely to become drawn and leggy – cleaning the greenhouse (or house) glazing will make a great difference, and standing the trays/pots on aluminium foil will reflect back some light.

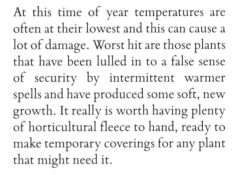

At this time of year temperatures are often at their lowest and this can cause a lot of damage. Worst hit are those plants that have been lulled in to a false sense of security by intermittent warmer spells and have produced some soft, new growth. It really is worth having plenty of horticultural fleece to hand, ready to make temporary coverings for any plant that might need it.

Fleece can be kept firmly in place using special fixing pegs. Alternatively, fashion your own from old galvanised metal coat hangers! If plants do get frosted, blackening of the foliage is a common symptom. Don't pinch, cut or prune this off unless it shows signs of deterioration or fungal growth – damaged old foliage can help to protect against the next onslaught of bitter cold!

Damping-off disease is caused by a range of pathogens, mainly water- or soil-borne fungi, and it causes seedlings to keel over and die, often becoming shrunken and discoloured at the base and sometimes showing an off-white fungal fuzziness once dead. It is quite impossible to control it once the seedling has been damaged, so it is an infection you need to do everything you possibly can to avoid! Using only clean mains water on seeds and seedlings, using properly cleaned trays, cells and pots and new, properly sterilised compost is the key to damping-off avoidance. It also helps if you avoid sowing the seeds too close together; mixing fine seed with equal quantities of dry, horticultural sand will make it much easier to sow fine seed adequately well-spaced. Overprotecting seedlings, by keeping them in a propagator for too long, will also encourage damping-off disease so, as soon as the seedlings are big enough, gradually harden them off and provide them with better air circulation and lower temperatures.

A serious garden and greenhouse tidy-up at this stage in the year can make a huge difference to pest and disease problems later on. Choose a mild day and clear everything you possibly can out of the greenhouse and cold frame.

If it is still a bit nippy, wrap plants in a couple of layers of fleece. Clear out all unnecessary items such as flowerpots, seed trays and old seed packets (as these can often harbour pests), scrub down the staging and glazing if you have not already done so and then dry off all surfaces as much as you can. As you replace plants and other items, give each a quick check over and remove any hibernating pests or deteriorating leaves. Then do a similar tidy-up in the garden, clearing overwintering snails from beneath pots and planters, and removing dead and damaged plants and old plant supports, all of which may well be harbouring problems. At the end you'll feel amazingly smug and the garden and greenhouse will look better… and most important of all, you'll have reduced the likelihood of problems occurring later in the year.

Notes

March

Early March

ORNAMENTALS

As soon as early flowering daffodils have finished flowering, remove the faded heads to encourage good results again next year. The dead heads make great compost, so don't waste them!

Start dividing established or overgrown clumps of herbaceous perennials such as helianthemums, day lilies and bergenias. Most herbaceous perennials benefit from a 'sort out' every few years: discard outer, decrepit sections and replant only vigorous inner sections.

Get flower beds and borders ready for the year ahead. Apply a general fertiliser to the soil between plants. Mulch with a garden compost, well-rotted manure or a proprietary compost or mulch mixture, and carefully remove any weeds from around existing plants. Take the opportunity to collect up any slugs that you find too.

Feed established shrubs, trees, climbers and roses and, if using a proprietary granular fertiliser, water in well unless rain is forecast. Choose either a special rose or flowering shrub feed, or a general fertiliser, depending on the plants being fed.

Prune climbing roses, floribundas and hybrid tea roses and check for signs of over-wintering black spot disease – prune out stems showing tiny purple black spots.

Make sure that seed potatoes are kept in a cool but frost-free and well-lit spot ready for planting. Ideally, put them in trays to 'chit' – this will generally mean you get a slightly earlier and somewhat heavier crop.

Plant out a few early potatoes now, putting them in pre-warmed soil and covering the row with a couple of layers of fleece or a fleece-covered pull-out tunnel. This will mean you can enjoy some superb new potatoes just that little bit earlier! Allow about 30 cm between each tuber, and plant each 12–15 cm deep.

Onion sets (mini onions) are available now. Plant them in a sunny, well-drained spot, using a trowel to create a small planting hole for each, and position them so that the neck of each bulb just protrudes above the soil. Allow 12–15 cm between each bulb, the bigger the spacing the larger the size of the bulb you harvest. Cover with chicken wire or netting to prevent birds pulling out the newly planted sets.

Apply sulphate of potash to the root area of all types of fruit bushes, canes and trees, then water in thoroughly and top up the mulch layer. This meal may not look exciting, but it will encourage fruit to crop more heavily.

Make sowings of early peas, beetroot, lettuce and chives.

If your lawn is full of moss and you're determined to fight it, apply a moss killer. Later in the month, once the moss is completely dead, you can rake it out but don't be tempted to do this straight away or you will spread the moss, making the problem worse. Get a spring-tined rake ready for the raking out.

If you want to create a new lawn from seed, get the ground prepared now – dig the area over thoroughly, removing large stones, weeds and debris, ready for sowing from late March onwards. If the ground is wet, wait until it dries out slightly. You can use the same preparation for a lawn created from turf.

Repair damaged edges and bare patches on lawns now, either using fresh grass seed or patches of turf. Make sure that the new seed or turf is of the same type and quality as the original, or else you may end up with a patchwork-quilt effect!

Early March is pretty well the last chance you'll have to plant bare-root trees and shrubs, or to create a new hedge from inexpensive bare-root transplants or seedlings. If you delay, the plants may not be available, or will have started to break in to leaf, so making success much less likely and aftercare much harder!

Late March

ORNAMENTALS

Sow seeds of hardy annual flowers into prepared areas of soil in a sunny spot. Many flowers can be sown direct, including flax, candytuft, nigella, cornflowers, poached egg flower, annual poppies, clarkia, lavatera, sweet sultan, sunflowers and larkspur.

Divide fleshy-rooted perennial flowers such as hostas and herbaceous peonies as soon as you see the new buds clearly. Keep the new sections well watered and mulched.

Many herbaceous flowers need support later on in the year, or they will flop! Make sure that you get twiggy sticks (thin sticks with branches), proprietary supports or canes in place now, well before they put on significant growth. It is much easier done early as there is less foliage to grapple with, and the plant is also less likely to get damaged.

Take cuttings from fuchsias and pelargoniums – this means you will have plenty of gorgeous new plants to brighten up beds, borders, hanging baskets, window boxes and tubs come summer, and all for an amazingly low cost.

Whilst the soil is still quite moist after the winter, apply or top-up mulches around the bases of anything that might conceivably benefit – trees, shrubs, climbers, all types of fruit too. The mulch should be about 8 cm or so deep and, ideally, cover the entire root-feeding area. Well-rotted manure, garden compost, leaf mould, proprietary mixes, composted bark and recycled compost from last year's containers all make good mulch. As soggy mulch can damage stems, make sure that whatever material you use is kept just clear of the stems or trunks.

As the soil starts to warm up ever so slightly it is worth starting to sow seeds of parsnips, parsley, lettuce, peas, leeks, chard, spinach, endive, beetroot, salad leaves and radish.

Plant strawberries, either in open ground or into pots, in a sunny spot. Choose a loam-based compost with added grit and water them in well. Cover existing strawberry plants with cloches or fleece to get an extra early crop. Plant out chitted (sprouted) tubers of early potatoes, provided the soil is not too soggy.

Continue to plant out chitted tubers of potatoes. Tubers do best in open ground, but you can often get a reasonable crop from container-grown potatoes too. Main-crop potatoes can be planted in warmer parts of the country and will need to be positioned with the 'rose' or blunt end uppermost with about 5 cm of soil on top of it. Main-crop varieties do take up considerably more space than 'earlies' – allow 35–38 cm between each tuber in the row and 70–75 cm between the rows.

Many small herb plants are now available in garden centres and nurseries, so why not plant up a container of your favourite culinary herbs? Use gritty compost and provide really good drainage by using large, chunky crocks (pieces of broken china or earthenware) in the base of the container.

Prick out and pot on any young plants of veg that you sowed earlier. Make sure that you handle the seedlings very carefully, never by the fragile stems. Water in well after moving each young plant to its new home.

Provided it is not too wet, mow the lawn – but make sure that the blades of the mower are set high, so that the grass is not cut too short. If the grass is already growing strongly you will need to mow regularly from now on – indeed, in some years mowing barely stops at any time of the year!

Keep on top of the weeds as this is the month when they start to appear and grow in earnest. Hoed off regularly, annual weeds can be kept under control pretty easily, but if you let them get out of hand now they will soon set seed and make for a lot more problems... potentially for years to come. Weeds that are not in flower or bearing seeds make great compost. Perennial weeds, such as dandelions, nettles and docks, are a different matter and as many have chunky and pernicious roots they are best removed in their entirety. You can safely compost leaves and stems, but don't add roots to the compost bin as they will survive and be spread around the garden with the compost.

Lawns are relatively easy to sow or create from turf at this time of year. When you choose the lawn seed mix or the turf, make sure you select one that is suitable for the site. Think about the wear it is likely to get and the look you are trying to achieve. There are special seed mixes for shaded areas, tough or hardwearing grasses, or at the other end of the extreme, the elegant bowling-green style! Remember: the finer the grasses, the more maintenance they tend to need.

Slugs and snails are one of the most damaging pests at this time of year. There is such a lot of soft, tender (and presumably very tasty) growth about, which slugs and snails can feast upon. Once plants start to get tougher they become less appetising and harder for the slimy pests to attack, so protection at these early stages is essential.

I'm a great fan of the biological control nematodes, available by mail/online, which can be watered on to the soil and are very efficient at killing off slugs (even the tiny black keeled slugs, which often work underground and cause so much devastation). Biological controls are totally safe for wildlife, pets, humans and other animals.

You can also create barriers around susceptible plants from a variety of widely available materials such as copper rings, sticky-backed copper tape (very useful on containers) and environmentally friendly slug treatments. Alternatively, use homemade or collected barriers such as crushed seashells, sharp grit, pine needles or even crushed egg shells. Damp and warm conditions often herald the arrival of slug and snail eggs too – small clusters of clear or milky white spheres, 1–2 mm in diameter, often to be found beneath deteriorating foliage or under pots.

It is not just slugs that start to make their presence felt at this time of year – just about every conceivable pest may well start to appear in March. So, grab a bag, a pair of secateurs and go on a regular bug hunt! It is amazing what you'll find; and if you pick off, prune out and collect up pests and also early signs of disease attack, you can often save yourself a lot of time later in the year… and of course save your plants from being nibbled, gnawed, grazed, infected or otherwise attacked. Bin or burn infected plant parts.

Some pests are not too worried about the conditions, but many others (including slugs, snails, vine weevils and earwigs) are far more likely to be spotted feasting upon your plants if you do your bug-hunting at dusk and, better still, after a spell of rain.

Whenever you choose to go looking for pests, make sure that you look deep within the branch or stem structure of all the plants, and that you always check the lower surface of the leaves too.

Notes

April

Early April

ORNAMENTALS

Plant summer-flowering bulbs such as lilies, ornamental alliums, gladioli, camassia, triteleia, eucomis and crocosmias in flower beds and borders. Lilies and alliums also do well in deep pots of well-drained compost and are a great way to brighten up patios and terraces later in the year.

It is time to spring-clean flower beds and borders! A simple tidy-up will make your garden look so much better and needn't cost you a penny! Collect up fallen twigs, rake up old leaves that have been redistributed over the winter, cut back dead and damaged leaves on perennials… and, unless diseased, add the whole lot to the compost bin.

Tie in stems of rambler and climbing roses, making sure that they are secure on their supports, but that there is also enough room for some stem expansion over the coming months. This needs to be done soon, as stems are still very flexible and so easier to deal with. Try to train as many as you can into the horizontal position as this will promote the formation of more side shoots, and so more blooms.

Prune forsythia and *Chaenomeles* (Japanese quince) as soon as they have finished flowering. On young plants you will need to leave some stems complete, as the plant still needs to increase in size, but pruning now will encourage more flowering next year. Forsythia stems that bore flowers should be pruned back to vigorous new outward-facing side shoots; with *Chaenomeles* prune the stems which have flowered back to just one or two healthy buds.

Earth up shoots on potatoes as soon as they emerge above ground – mounding soil on to the rows will prevent them suffering from frost damage. This will also help to ensure that the crop of new tubers forms deep enough in the soil for them to avoid turning green and becoming poisonous.

Sow some calabrese or broccoli, ideally one seed per cell of good quality compost. You need not have a greenhouse or propagator, as the seeds will germinate on a well-lit windowsill, providing the soil is kept just moist at all times.

Vegetables seedlings from seed sown last month may now be 6–8 cm tall, and in need of some fresh compost. Pot cell-grown or tray-grown plants into small individual pots of fresh compost.

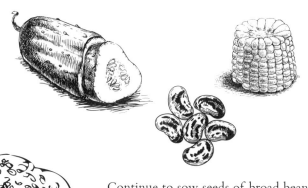

Continue to sow seeds of broad beans, lettuce, peas, rocket and salad leaves direct into a well-prepared soil into which you have forked well-rotted manure or garden compost. The best way to ensure a good, regular stream of these crops is to sow little and often. This 'successional sowing', at about two-week intervals, should produce crops for months on end. Make sure that the seed packets are resealed and kept in a cool, dry place after each sowing.

Water fruit trees, canes and bushes regularly, especially if the weather is gusty or dry. Any fruit that was planted within the last eighteen months or so will be especially vulnerable to drought damage, as it will not yet have become fully established, so these are the real priority. Keep the soil around the base of all fruit plants free from weeds – regular hoeing is the easiest way to keep annual weeds down. Once weeded, top up mulch levels if necessary.

Water features often become pretty grim after the winter – with dead algae, new algae, fallen leaves and other debris clogging them up and discolouring the water – so empty them out now. Use a stiff brush to scrub them out and then rinse with clean water before refilling with clean water.

There should be a good selection of pond plants readily available now, and it is a great time to add to existing pond and marginal plantings, or to add to ponds which could do with denser planting. Make sure that new plants are suitable for the depth of water that you have available; planted too deep or too shallow, pond and marginal plants are often quick to fail. Check plant labels for specific planting depths.

Coarse grasses can ruin the appearance of your lawn. One of the best ways to deal with them without too much effort is to grab a rake and fluff up the patches of tough grasses just before you mow – this raises them up from their normal position and makes it more likely that they will be cut back by the mower blades.

Lawns and indeed all grass is likely to need much more frequent mowing now that the weather has warmed up; if left to grow too long it is much harder cut back well, and the lawn will often look awful after cutting, so regular mowing now needs to feature on your to-do list!

Late April

ORNAMENTALS

Why not have a lovely day out – visit a favourite nursery or garden centre and treat yourself to a selection of pretty alpines, a shallow trough or other container, some gritty compost… and plant up a delightful miniature alpine garden.

Keep spring-flowering bulbs in good condition by feeding them now. Apply a general fertiliser around individual bulbs or larger clumps, whether they are growing in beds and borders or naturalised in grass. Rake the fertiliser in gently or, on grassed areas, just water in thoroughly. If bulbs have not been fed for several years, foliar feed them by applying suitable liquid feed to the leaves while the foliage is still green.

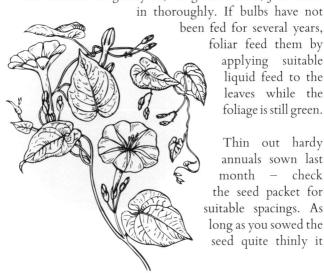

Thin out hardy annuals sown last month – check the seed packet for suitable spacings. As long as you sowed the seed quite thinly it should not be too time-consuming. Remove the weaker-looking seedlings or any that have been damaged. If you do the thinning out carefully, you can always transplant those seedlings that you weed out, and use them to brighten up another bit of spare ground. After thinning, water the whole area well to resettle the soil around the plant roots.

Harden off sweet-pea seedlings and get them planted out into a sunny spot where you intend them to flower. Why not make a wigwam from bamboo canes and string, or a support from twiggy pea sticks, or allow some to scramble over existing shrubs or trellis?

Sow some morning glory seeds. Soak the seeds in water for a few hours and then sow them into good quality compost. These are best sown right at the end of this month, or even in early May, as they are very intolerant of cold and their growth is easily checked if they are planted out too early.

Continue to sow seeds of beans, courgettes, sweetcorn and outdoor tomatoes. In mild areas they can be sown direct into the garden soil outside, but if in doubt sow into small pots (root trainers for the sweetcorn) or trays.

Continue to plant main-crop seed potatoes. Plant each tuber with the blunt or 'rose' end uppermost so that it has about 5 cm of soil above it and with 35–38 cm between the tubers, and 70–75 cm between the rows.

Plant out any remaining greenhouse tomatoes or pepper plants now, either into their final pots or planters or into the greenhouse border soil.
If you have a conservatory or sunny porch, this too could be a good home for a pepper or tomato plant!

Make more successional sowings of vegetable and herb seeds direct in to garden soil, watering well.

This is usually the latest you can leave it if you want to order in any garden-ready vegetable plants, so make sure that you do this now as it can be a great way to make up for lost time or catch up on the seed-sowing you never quite managed to do!

Regularly hand-weed or hoe around vegetable seedlings that are starting to come up – weeds create a lot of competition for food and moisture and can cause serious setbacks to seedlings. An 'onion hoe' has a very small head and is great for weeding in tight spaces.

Regularly check ponds for blanket weed and duckweed and remove every trace if you find any. Allowed to grow unchecked, both weeds can literally clog up the water and cover the surface of the pond too. An old kitchen sieve makes a great tool for skimming off duckweed, and a sturdy bamboo cane or garden rake can both be used to drag out developing masses of blanket weed.

Give your lawn a bit of a treat after the winter and apply a spring lawn fertiliser. If you use a granular formulation it will need to be watered in promptly after application. This can be done by hand or, ideally, save yourself some time and plan the application of the fertiliser so that you get it on just before rain is due.

Check all climbing and twining plants and re-tie-in if necessary. Some may have been dislodged during the winter and some may have put on new growth. Tying shoots into a horizontal position tends to encourage more flowering.

Blitz lawn weeds – carefully remove them with a kitchen knife, digging out the entire root system if possible, or on larger areas consider using a lawn weedkiller, but do apply it precisely according to the manufacturer's instructions to avoid accidental damage to garden plants.

TIPS FOR *April*

WEATHER DAMAGE

Even though it may feel like spring has arrived, don't forget that your garden may still be hit by a late frost or two. The soft, tender new growth that is developing on just about everything is especially prone to cold damage. You may also find that weather-damage caused over the last couple of months also becomes more obvious, now that it is surrounded by lush new growth.

Symptoms vary a lot from plant to plant, but discolouration – especially the development of dark brown or black areas or entire leaves – and dieback are very common. Some of the tougher plants may even be damaged, and on these you may see a peculiar bagginess beneath the leaf, almost as if the outermost layer of the leaf is too big for the leaf itself, and often combined with some distortion.

Check weather forecasts regularly and, using your local knowledge as well, provided that you can be pretty confident that the worst of the weather is definitely over, prune out damaged areas now.

APHIDS

Greenfly, blackfly and just about every conceivable colour of aphid are likely to be doing a lot of damage this month. Like most other pests, they are especially fond of soft, succulent plant foliage; they feed by sucking plant sap and may cause a range of symptoms including yellowing, distortion (especially puckering), dieback and general stunting. As aphids are unable to digest all the sugars the sap contains, their excreta is itself sugary and is known as 'honey dew' – this may also give aphid-infested plants (and their neighbours) a sticky texture.

Sometimes the honey dew attracts black mould growth, and this sooty mould covers the plants too. Aphids may also spread plant viruses as they feed and move from plant to plant – so, all in all, you can see why they may need to be controlled! Hand-squashing, jetting them off sturdier plants with a strong blast of water or, if necessary, a treatment with plant oil may work. Plant oil is available from garden centres, websites and catalogues, as are soft soaps or soft soap solution, which all work well. I also try to encourage aphid-feeding birds into the area by hanging up bird feeders close by.

Notes

May

Early May

ORNAMENTALS

Treat yourself and your pond to a water lily or maybe even several! Provided it is planted at the correct depth it should look great for years to come and the surface-floating foliage helps to shade the water, so cutting down on the build-up of algae.

If you have a cold greenhouse or good-sized porch, plant up hanging baskets and other summer bedding containers now, then keep them in the greenhouse or porch until the last frosts are over (usually late May or early June). If you do not have somewhere like this that will protect tender plants from frost, avoid the temptation of the summer bedding plants that are often for sale by now – they're likely to get damaged or even killed if left outside during a frost.

Empty out containers that were used for winter bedding displays. Avoid re-using the old compost as, although it might be tempting to do so, if you do this you are more likely to end up with problems such as vine weevil!

Make sure that all herbaceous perennials that benefit from a bit of a support system have one in place. Add extra twiggy pea sticks if you underestimated a plant's needs when you first put the supports in earlier in the year.

Cut back and neaten up some of the earlier flowering herbaceous perennials such as *Doronicum*, *Dicentra*, pulmonarias if they have finished flowering. A quick sort out now will help to remove any mildew, and may also encourage a few more flowers to appear.

Continue to earth up potatoes; this will need to be repeated every week or so as the top-growth is now developing fast. As you mound up the soil over the emerging shoots, take the opportunity to remove any weeds too.

Thin out seedlings of direct-sown vegetables as necessary and make further sowings of vegetables suggested last month. The spacing required varies dramatically from crop to crop, and sometimes even with the variety you've selected, so always check the seed packet for details. After thinning, water the row thoroughly so that the soil resettles and the young vegetable plants will be less likely to suffer dryness at the roots.

Make sure that sowings of carrots are covered with fleece to prevent carrot fly damage. Alternatively, treat yourself to a very fine mesh- or fleece-covered pull-out tunnel, which is easy to put over the row and remove and replace for weeding and harvesting.

There is still time to sow seeds of French beans, runner beans, courgettes, marrows, sweetcorn, squash and pumpkins into individual pots or cells. Keep the seedlings on a warm windowsill or in a greenhouse and ensure the compost is always just moist, and you'll be amazed at how fast they grow!

Mow the lawn regularly, removing clippings and adding them to the compost bin in small quantities. However, if drought is forecast you can allow short clippings to remain on the lawn, as in dry weather they may help to reduce drought damage.

Remove bubble-wrap polythene and other insulating materials from around outdoor pots and planters. In the coldest regions of the country, or if very cold weather is forecast, wait a few weeks before you do this… just in case!

Continue to tie in fast-growing climbers as necessary. I use garden twine for lightweight plants, or for a longer-lasting system and for heavier weight stems try foam-covered wire, as this has more strength and the foam helps to reduce the risk of the wire cutting in to the stem.

Gradually acclimatise plants that you brought into a protected spot or sheltered area, or which you protected with a fleece or similar covering for the winter. Take them out during the day and then cover them or bring back under protection at night.

You really cannot pause from weeding at this time of year – just think how much work you'll be saving yourself each time you hoe off a weed before it has a chance to set seed. They do say that, 'One year's seed is seven years' weed!'

Late May

ORNAMENTALS

Unless frosts are forecast, it should be safe to plant out or display summer bedding now. Planters and display pots that have been grown in a greenhouse will need to be acclimatised to life in the garden for several days first. If there is a sudden cold spell, cover them in fleece until it warms up again. If some of the plants are bearing quite a few flowers it may seem difficult to do, but if you pinch off the flowers at planting, the plant will establish better and end up producing a better show. Be firm!

Plant up containers with summer bedding flowers – if you did not grow any yourself there will still be plenty of varieties to choose from in your local garden centres. Always use good quality compost, and if you incorporate

some controlled-release fertiliser granules this will reduce the frequency of feeding over the coming months. It is amazing just how many more plants you can use in a container than you might think; provided the container is well fed and watered, you can really cram the plants in (but gently of course!).

Continue to thin out sowings of hardy annual flowers made earlier in the year, following instructions on the seed packet for final spacings. Water in well after thinning out. Sunflowers will grow upwards extremely fast, and it really is worth supplying each with some support whilst the stems are still flimsy.

Continue to sow runner bean and climbing French bean seeds direct in to the garden, or plant out young plants and then train them up a wigwam of sticks or bamboo canes. Add a few small sweet-pea plants for extra colour and delightful perfume and you'll find that the wigwam not only looks prettier, but the sweet-pea flowers attract pollinators too!

Gradually harden off and then plant out vegetables sown earlier, watering them in well if the weather is dry. If in any doubt about the weather, be prepared to cover young plants with a layer or two of fleece. Keep the fleece well secured using bricks, large stones or metal pegs around the edges. Hardening off means allowing the plants to remain outside during the day, then bringing them under cover at night (using fleece day or night, if need be, to give extra protection) and gradually reducing the protection given over a period of a week or so. This allows the plants to become acclimatised to life in the garden.

In more sheltered and warmer parts of the country, you can now start to plant out outdoor varieties of tomato, hardening each plant off carefully before you do so. Make sure that you have mini cloches or plenty of fleece to hand, just in case the weather turns again.

Plant yourself a few productive pots – how about some chilli peppers, sweet peppers or maybe even a selection of your favourite salad vegetables? A large container (at least 30 sq. cm) is easier to maintain than a small one, and even bigger is even easier! Lots of other vegetables grow well in good-sized planters too, such as dwarf French beans, tomatoes, salad leaves and lettuces, French beans, aubergines and herbs.

Make regular checks for greenfly and blackfly – they infest pretty well everything and should be controlled promptly if you don't want to end up with a lot more of these sap-suckers than you've got at the moment! For more details on pest control see Tips for April.

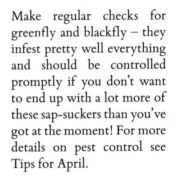

If you sowed a lawn from seed earlier this year then it should now be ready to have its first cut; as long as the individual blades of grass are at least 5 cm in height, it is ready. Set the mower blades as high as possible and go really gently. If there is even the slightest sign of the young grass being uprooted rather than cut, stop! Either the mower needs to be sharpened or you need to delay mowing a week or two longer.

If the weather is dry remember that mulching over a moist soil helps conserve moisture, so saving the plants some serious stress, and you some time. For best results the mulch should go on to a moist soil and be 5–8 cm deep, applied in a large area beneath the main stem or trunk, ideally out as far as the spread of the outermost branches. This means it should cover the entire rooting area – if something this extensive is not feasible then mulch what you can, as this will still be better than nothing!

WATERING

With conditions likely to be drier than ever this month, and likely to stay that way for a good while, it is time to think about watering and water conservation. If possible, install water-butts with a down pipe from the guttering of every roof you own; even a shed roof can help to build up water supplies during wet spells.

If the garden needs water then try to apply it last thing in the afternoon or in the early evening or, failing that, first thing in the morning. If soil has been dry for a while when you do water it, there is a tendency for the water to run straight off the surface and away from where it is needed most. Try lightly sprinkling the soil surface and then returning to thoroughly water the area 20 minutes or so later.

It is better, and more useful to the plants, if you water less frequently and more thoroughly, getting water deep into the soil. Lighter watering often only wets the upper areas of the soil, which is rarely where the roots are – and it may actually encourage the plant roots to stay near the soil's surface where they will then be more likely to suffer drought damage.

BLACKSPOT OF ROSES

This fungal infection causes purple-black blotches on the foliage of roses; each blotch has spidery or uneven edges and, as the blotches increase in size, they often coalesce. Infected leaves soon yellow and fall, so the rose may well be seriously weakened, especially if the infection occurs for several years in succession or hits early in the year. Keep a close watch on roses from now on and try to pick off any early infections. If it gets out of hand, then consider spraying with a suitable fungicide. As the infected leaves fall, clear them up and dispose of them as this will significantly reduce potential attacks next year.

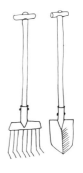

A feed with a good general fertiliser or a special rose fertiliser will help to boost the plant's vigour, but do not apply this any later than the end of next month. In the spring it is worth carefully pruning out any stems showing small purple-black blotches as these may be the overwintering black spot, just waiting to cause problems! There are lots of other fungal leaf spots which may attack a wide range of garden plants, but rose blackspot only attacks roses, so no need to worry about it attacking other garden favourites.

Notes

June

Early June

ORNAMENTALS

Give early flowering herbaceous perennials a 'haircut' – cutting these back as soon as flowering is over will encourage a second, later flush of flowers towards the end of summer. All you need to do is remove the faded flowers, plus a little of the growth beneath, then keep the plant well fed and watered and you should be well rewarded a few weeks later. You'll also find that this helps to keep the plants dense too.

Plan ahead to fill your garden with some favourite flowers and sow seeds of hardy perennial and biennial flowers such as verbascums, wallflowers, Sweet Williams, Canterbury bells. If the seed is sown shortly, these will be ready to flower next year.

Use a sharp pair of secateurs to prune *Philadelphus* (mock orange), spiraeas, *Syringa* (lilac), *Buddleja alternifolia*, weigela, *Ribes sanguineum*, *Kolkwitzia*, deciduous cotoneaster, *Exochorda* and *Deutzia* after flowering.

If you are planning to do any major planting later in the year in areas that contain quite a few bulbs, it is well worth marking any clumps of bulbs before the foliage dies away completely. Come the autumn, when the leaves of the bulbs are no longer there, you'll be amazed how useful the markers are and they can save you a lot of time as you won't be constantly digging up and replanting bulbs!

Regularly deadhead spring- and summer-flowering bedding and herbaceous plants – if left to form seedheads the plant's vigour may be considerably reduced. Faded flowers also make great compost, so won't be wasted!

It should now be safe to plant out vegetables that you have raised yourself or bought from a garden centre, even if you live in one of the coldest parts of the country. Make sure everything is hardened off properly before planting out, and keep them well watered.

Continue to earth up potatoes, carefully drawing the soil up from between the rows and mounding it over the foliage as it emerges. If you made early plantings then it is also worth a check below ground on first early varieties – some may be ready for eating.

Regular watering may be essential, even if you've prepared your vegetable plot soil well. Try to keep this to a minimum, but remember that some vegetables, such as lettuce and coriander and spinach, are very prone to bolt or running to seed if water is in short supply, and others such as beans and peas will often fail to set a decent number of pods in dry conditions, so these need to be top priority when it comes to using available supplies of water.

Crops such as tomatoes, peppers and aubergines all need regular feeding with a liquid high-potash feed at this time of year. Without this the level of cropping is often dramatically reduced. I use a liquid tomato feed for all of these 'fruiting' crops.

Take a few minutes to remove faded flowers from marginal plants, such as marsh marigold, growing around your pond; this helps to encourage more flowering later in the year and will reduce the amount of debris that falls from the plant and then rots down in the water.

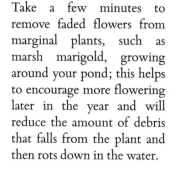

Continue to mow your lawn regularly – in most areas this means twice a week, but this obviously depends on local conditions and the weather. Small quantities of clippings can be incorporated into your compost heap, or use a special activator to convert them into useful compost.

As the weather warms up and the sun gets brighter, temperatures can rise dangerously high under glass, increasing the risk of scorching on plant foliage and flowers in greenhouses and frames. Apply a shading paint or install blinds on greenhouses to keep this in check. Remember to keep vents and windows open as much as possible too.

This is a good time to introduce a few floating plants, such as water lilies, to your pond. Establishment should be rapid and there is no risk of cold damage to tender growth. These plants will not only look good but will also help save you time – by lying flat on the pond's surface they create a good amount of shade, dramatically reducing the growth of algae, blanket weed and the 'pea soup' green pond we all dread.

Late June

ORNAMENTALS

Be brave and take the shears to aubrieta, perennial candytuft and arabis after they have finished flowering – this keeps the plants compact and flowering well for longer in the season and prevents them from becoming straggly.

Tie in wall shrubs and climbers to their supports now while the stems are still fairly pliable, training as many as you can close to the horizontal position, to maximise flower-bud production.

Sow winter-flowering pansies and polyanthus if you would like some low-cost, high-impact colour for your garden early next year.

Continue to sow seeds of favourite herbaceous perennials such as alpine poppies, hollyhocks, Oriental and Iceland poppies, lupins, aubrieta, anchusa, delphinium, foxgloves, geum, campanulas and erigeron.

Feed summer-flowering container plants regularly with a liquid tomato fertiliser to encourage good flowering; if the compost has become too dry, water lightly first before applying the feed. Regularly deadhead flowers, too, as this hugely increases their flowering potential.

Use secateurs or shears to clip brooms to prevent them becoming leggy, but if this is a job you've not done regularly before, only cut back the more recent growth.

Remove suckers from roses as they appear; these growths are produced from the rootstocks of the rose and, as they are generally far more vigorous than the rest of the plant, if left in place they may seriously weaken the rose. Suckers usually have a leaf with a different shape and may be slightly paler in colour. Try to remove them by pulling firmly.

Continue to sow salad seeds, such as lettuce, rocket, beetroot and radish, either in containers or in open ground. Water them and then cover with a mesh or similar material to keep the birds and cats away.

Early varieties of potato should be ready to harvest now (if you've not already had a few sneaky meals!). If you choose a dry day (and one when the soil is starting to dry out), you will save yourself a lot of time, as the soil will be far less likely to adhere to the tubers on lifting. Remember that the foliage of new potato plants does not need to be yellowed before you start to harvest. If you are not sure whether the tubers are ready or not, carefully scoop away the soil at the base of one plant and check the size of the tubers – if they are still too small, wait a week or two before checking again.

Continue to regularly remove side shoots from tomato plants that are not of the bush type – this means most of the greenhouse varieties. Hold the side shoot firmly between your finger and thumb and hold the main stem in the other hand, then snap out the side shoot by swiftly bending it downwards.

Feed tomatoes, peppers and aubergines with a dilute high-potash feed, such as a tomato feed, every week or two to encourage plenty more flowers and good-sized fruits.

In dry weather your lawn may still need to be cut, but don't forget that slightly longer grass is generally more drought-resistant than a lawn cut very short, so set the mower blades high.

Keep weeding all areas of your garden as often as you can – less established weeds are so much easier to remove without disturbing neighbouring plants, and you will also have fewer problems with weed seeds forming.

As temperatures rise you may need to top up ponds and water features occasionally. Water levels may drop dramatically at this time of year, due to evaporation and use by local wildlife, and if levels are plummeting it may be wise to check for leaks.

If your pond is turning bright green this is likely to be due to a massive growth of algae in the water, something often encouraged by warmer weather. Do not be tempted to change the water, as with fresh hose-water the pond will take a while to rebalance itself. Instead, don't forget the benefit of adding more oxygenator plants and surface floaters, and consider adding some bundles of barley straw – a pair of old tights makes a perfect container for the straw, weighed down with a brick or two. Barley straw pads are also available from garden centres and mail order suppliers if you do not have access to straw, but both help to banish the algae.

CATERPILLARS

Holes nibbled in leaves, often accompanied by tiny blackish-brown cubes of 'frass' or droppings, suggest that caterpillars are about. Many feed in the evenings and so the best time to spot the culprit is generally at dusk or maybe even a little later. Caterpillars are a really common pest and just about every plant is likely to suffer attacks from them on occasion. Avoid contact with any hairy caterpillars as these often cause allergic or other dangerous reactions.

With edible crops it is often feasible to use fine mesh or fleece to form a barrier around the plants, so that the adults (butterflies and moths) cannot lay their eggs in the first place. There is a great range of suitable materials, and some covered pull-out tunnels that are really effective. You could also consider treating the infestation with a biological control, as this will kill off the caterpillars without posing any threat to other animals.

POWDERY MILDEWS

Powdery mildews almost always appear as a white or off-white powdery coating on leaves, stems, buds or flowers. This is then often followed by distortion or puckering of the leaves, yellowing and premature leaf drop. A fairly severe attack of powdery mildew early in the season can cause serious weakening of the plant, especially if the mildew strikes several years in succession.

There are numerous different fungi that cause powdery mildew diseases and almost all garden plants may be affected. Powdery mildew fungi tend to cause most damage when the air around a plant is moist and when the soil around the plant's roots is dry, so always try to keep the soil adequately watered and mulched, and improve air circulation around the stems and foliage, perhaps by careful pruning. If the infection appears it is also worth picking off or even pruning out the worst affected areas. If mildew is a recurrent problem, especially with edible crops, consider growing relatively resistant varieties if these are available; also consider spraying with a suitable fungicide.

Notes

July

Early July

ORNAMENTALS

Continue to regularly deadhead herbaceous perennials and summer bedding plants to encourage more flowers and prolong the flowering period. It may seem like a never-ending job, but it really does make a world of difference!

As soon as columbines *(Aquilegia)* have finished flowering and have formed ripe seed heads, pick off a few of the seed heads and sprinkle the seeds into the soil in a vacant part of the garden. They germinate and grow very readily and rapidly and make a wonderful flower for filling gaps and introducing much-needed colour.

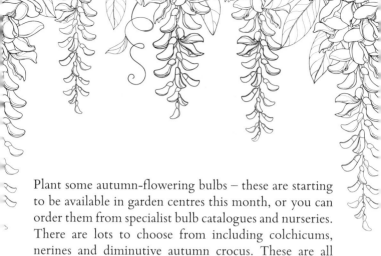

Plant some autumn-flowering bulbs – these are starting to be available in garden centres this month, or you can order them from specialist bulb catalogues and nurseries. There are lots to choose from including colchicums, nerines and diminutive autumn crocus. These are all reliable performers and should last for years and years, gradually building up their numbers in time. Choose a sunny, well-drained spot for best results.

Both dahlias and sweet peas will be flowering their socks off this month. The best way to ensure that they continue to do so, producing a maximum number of blooms for as long a period as possible, is to keep picking the flowers really frequently, so add a vase or two to your kitchen table.

Prick out seedlings of perennials and biennials, transplanting them into larger pots and then into a nursery bed. Water well.

As soon as the foliage of garlic and onions starts to yellow and flop, they will soon be ready to harvest. I like to eat some of the crop as soon as it has a decent-sized bulb (it is incredibly tasty and succulent!) but the majority of bulbs need to be stored. Use a fork to gently ease the bulbs from the soil and allow them to dry off thoroughly on the soil surface for a few days. Store in a cool, well-ventilated place.

Continue to remove the side shoots from tomatoes. This can seem like a never-ending chore, but it does prevent the plants becoming too wild and bushy, and also less productive. Pinching out side shoots helps to keep the vigour centred on the main part of the plant, and on the trusses it already has in place.

Continue to lift and enjoy early potatoes as soon as they are ready. If the foliage appears perfectly healthy it can be composted, but if it looks even the slightest bit discoloured or sickly, bin or burn it.

Make sowings of your favourite salad crops. What you choose is up to you – perhaps some lettuce, claytonia, lamb's lettuce, beetroot, spinach and rocket. If you are sowing purely for use as salad leaves, you can sow the seed much closer than if you were after full-sized plants, as you are likely to harvest the crop before it struggles for space.

Don't panic if the lawn turns brown during dry weather. Unless it was recently sown or laid it will re-green as soon as the weather gets wetter again; most turf grasses are amazingly resilient.

This is usually the beginning of the main season for eating outside in the garden. When selecting garden lighting, why not include a few candles containing citronella, as many people swear by its ability to keep the mosquitoes and midges away.

Regularly hose off garden furniture, especially tables, to remove all traces of food or drink spillages – this way you are less likely to see quite so many wasps!

Take every opportunity to check all your plants for pests and diseases. There's no need to become totally neurotic, but these regular checks can stop a problem from getting completely out of hand. Early infestations are so much easier to deal with, and less likely to spoil the overall appearance and performance of the plant.

Trim hedges regularly to encourage good dense growth of the general hedge structure. At this time of year there is unlikely to be any nesting bird problems, but I'd still suggest a quick check before you start.

Late July

ORNAMENTALS

Deadhead roses promptly to keep them blooming and prevent flowers deteriorating in damp weather – a sharp pair of secateurs is perfect for the job; just cut off the faded flower and flower stalks. Disease-free dead heads make great compost.

Feed all your roses with a special rose fertiliser, formulated to encourage both good growth and great flowering, as a reward for flowering so well. If you use a dry formulation, make sure you water it in well.

If you're in a warmer part of the country, summer prune wisterias to encourage flowering. Shorten the often rather long and whippy side growths on the main stems to six leaves each. On a large wisteria this can take quite a while, but it is worth it as it will encourage the formation of plenty of new flower buds, ready for next year.

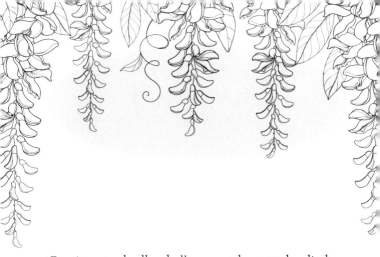

Continue to deadhead all perennials, annuals, climbers
and shrubs as regularly as possible. I suggest carrying a
pair of sharp secateurs around with you whenever you
garden, that way you will always have them to hand
ready to tackle the dead heads.

Divide over-congested clumps of rhizomatous iris, as
once these have been established for a few years they
soon stop performing as they should. Lift each clump
with a fork and, with a sharp knife, divide the rhizome
into sections, only saving and replanting the healthiest-
looking pieces.

Plant out leeks and cauliflowers sown earlier or bought by mail order, watering them in well to settle the soil around the roots. Make sure that the cauliflowers are extremely well firmed into the soil.

Pinch out or cut off the main leading shots on runner beans and climbing French beans that have reached the top of their supports. This will help to encourage more side shoots to be produced lower down on the plants, and so should mean more delicious beans.

Trim back over-exuberant growth on herbs using scissors or shears, depending on the size of the plant. This helps to prevent them becoming straggly and also encourages new growth and bushiness. Any trimmings that look good can be chopped and frozen in ice cube trays with a little water – a useful way of preserving fresh herbs to use later in the year.

Prune your summer-fruiting raspberries as soon as you have enjoyed the last of this year's harvest. Cut all those canes that have borne fruit this year to within about 5 cm of ground level and leave the more flexible young, greener-looking canes in place, as you will then need to select the best-looking seven or so of these to be tied into the support system, ready to crop next year.

Water all plants in containers regularly, ensuring that the moisture penetrates right down to the base of the container – in hot weather this may mean twice a day, sometimes more! If necessary, move some plants into a slightly cooler position so that they are not in direct sun. Grouping containers together so that they provide some shade for each other will also help to reduce heat stress.

Lawns laid or sown earlier this year or last autumn may look lovely by now, but they will still be less well-established than an old lawn, so during periods of very dry weather an occasional but very thorough watering will be a good idea. Older lawns can be left to their own devices.

Provided the grass is not drought stressed, and the soil beneath it is slightly moist, consider applying a lawn feed. Choose one formulated for summer use and ensure that if you use a dry formulation you water it in really well to avoid any risk of scorching.

A regular pest patrol is still essential, so take a few minutes to have a wander around your garden.

TOMATO BLIGHT

Tomatoes, when grown outside, are very prone to attack by *Phytophthora infestans*, the potato blight fungus. This causes greyish-black blotches to develop on the stems and leaves, often combined with wilting and dieback. The plants look almost as if someone has zapped them with a blowtorch. The fruits are usually attacked when they are still green, but symptoms are most obvious once they have started to ripen. Gingery-brown or blackish-brown discolouration develops on the fruits and spreads within the flesh, and the fruits are then likely to be attacked by secondary rots, soon becoming completely inedible.

The best solution is to grow tomatoes in a greenhouse or frame. There are blight-resistant varieties on the market, but they might still succumb anyway!

The fungus responsible also attacks potatoes, and similar symptoms develop on the leaves and stems of these. If you see this, it is essential that you cut back the top-growth promptly, so that the spores cannot be washed down and infect the tubers. As soon as weather permits you should then lift the crop of tubers.

Infected plant parts are highly contagious and should be bagged up and binned or burned as quickly as possible, never composted.

SEMI-RIPE CUTTINGS

If you can spare the time, why not indulge in a little semi-ripe propagation? You can take cuttings material from your own plants, or even ask friends and neighbours for some material too. Choose a healthy shoot, use a sharp knife to cut it off just above a node, remove any side shoots and trim back the main stem to just below a node, leaving a cutting 10–15 cm long. Remove the lowermost few leaves and cut out any very soft growth right at the tip. Next, dip the base in some hormone rooting powder, tap off the excess and place each cutting in a small pot of gritty cuttings compost.

Rooting the cutting in a heated propagator will speed up the process, but they should also root in a cold frame. Keep the compost just moist at all times. If using a frame, enclose each pot in a miniature cloche or clear polythene bag. Once the cutting is well rooted you will be able to put it into a larger pot, harden it off and then grow it on in the garden.

Semi-ripe cuttings work really well for the following shrubs: aucuba, skimmia, rhododendron, berberis, carpenteria, cotoneaster, photinia, lavender, pieris, ceanothus, elaeagnus and escallonia.

Notes

August

Early August

ORNAMENTALS

Collect up diseased leaves from beneath roses and other shrubs, trees and climbers. If the foliage has fallen at this time of year (unless the plant is seriously drought-stressed) there's a high chance that the leaves are infected with a disease such as rust, mildew or leaf spot. By collecting them up you can help to reduce disease problems in the future.

Continue to deadhead plants in beds and borders unless of course it is a rose or other plant that you grow for its autumn hips.

As soon as the flowers on lavender have faded, give the entire plant a trim with shears or scissors, removing the faded blooms and a little of the stem beneath. The plant may look a little cut-about at first, but will soon recover and be more inclined to keep a dense shape.

If you are out for more than a day at a time and the weather is very hot, consider taking hanging baskets down from their supports, and moving pots and planters to a slightly more shaded spot.

Snip off foliage on some of your chives, cutting back to 8–10 cm above the crown of the plant. This will help to encourage new growth for use in late autumn and, if weather permits, maybe even in early winter too.

Continue to keep vegetable plants well watered. Water in the early evening if at all possible. Top up mulches if necessary.

Keep on harvesting as often as you can – it really is true that the more you pick the more you get, especially with vegetables such as courgettes, marrows, peas and beans.

Once you are sure that onions and garlic lifted earlier on are completely dry, hang the bulbs up to store in a dry, well ventilated spot away from any direct heat source.

Watch out for brown rot infection on developing fruit and remove damaged and rotting fruits as promptly as you can.

Summer prune cordon and espalier apple and pear trees to ensure they keep growing where you need them to. At the same time, prune out any diseased or damaged branches.

Keep weeding regularly so weeds do not get a chance to compete with or swamp flowers or vegetables. They still grow phenomenally fast at this time of year, especially if there has been rain or you have been watering the garden. Most annual weeds can easily be hoed off, and if you do this during the heat of the day or just before you can leave the weeds on the soil surface where they will frazzle up and die.

If you are about to go on holiday, persuade a friend, relative or neighbour to pop in from time to time to check your garden and keep your houseplants watered. Plants in pots or other containers are often most at risk, especially if the weather is hot. Alternatively, set up a drip or trickle irrigation system.

When you water your garden, give the pond and any water features a bit of a watering too. This will help top up and replenish lost moisture, but just as important, the droplets will help to introduce oxygen, so making it a better environment for pond wildlife and plants, also helping to reduce problems with algae.

Continue to remove duckweed and blanket weed from ponds and water features, remembering to leave blanket weed resting at the side of the pond for a few days before composting it, so that any entangled wildlife has a chance to escape back into the pond.

Late August

ORNAMENTALS

Think ahead and order spring-flowering bulbs or visit your local garden centre and see what they have available. Spring-flowering bulb planting starts next month, so make sure you have some lovely spring potential to get in to your garden.

Prune rambler roses as soon as they have finished flowering; cut back side shoots that bore flowers to one or two buds from the main stem. Next, remove any dead, damaged or spindly growth, and finally tie in the new, vigorous stems, making sure you spread these out well and tie in firmly, but with a little slack to allow for the stems to thicken up.

Be tough – collect up and compost any annuals that have definitely passed their best and have no chance of getting their strength back up to perform again. Annuals that are still looking fine will benefit from a bit of a liquid high-potash feed – this may perk them up enough to give you just a few more flowers.

Treat yourself to a few really special bulbs, such as the Madonna lily. These stunning flowers need a warm, sunny spot with a well-drained soil if they are to show their full potential. They should be available in catalogues and garden centres now.

Continue to keep a close watch on tomatoes and potatoes and remove any showing signs of blight infection (see Tips for July) – remember, they must be binned or burned promptly, not composted.

If tomatoes growing in the greenhouse have become very leafy, remove some of the foliage – a maximum of one-fifth – as this will allow a little more light through to the fruits so that they can ripen well, but not restrict the plant's ability to feed itself.

Don't forget to order some garden-ready vegetable plants of overwintering crops such as cauliflowers, sprouting broccoli and cabbage. These can then be planted in spaces left by summer crops.

If tomatoes are showing splitting on the fruits, this suggests erratic watering. If picked promptly these split fruits still make good eating, but try to reduce the problem by keeping the soil or compost moist at all times.

As soon as the golden 'silks' protruding from the top of sweetcorn cobs turn brown, the cobs may be ripe. But before harvesting any carefully push back the greenery covering the cob, and check that the kernels within are pale or golden yellow… enjoy!

Earlier cropping apples may be ripening well now. Check that the fruit is ready to be picked by carefully cupping each one in your hand and giving it a twist, if the fruit comes away it is ripe, if it doesn't you'll have to wait a while longer.

Apply a moss killer to the lawn if the weather is damp, and if you really feel you cannot bear the moss and will not manage to control it by improving your general lawn care.

If you have plans to lay or sow a new lawn this autumn, then start the soil preparation now. By doing this a good few weeks in advance of the actual sowing or laying, you will have the chance to rake off at least one batch of weeds before the seed or turf is in place… and it is much easier to weed bare soil than an area of emerging grass or newly laid turf.

Cut back or trim deciduous and coniferous hedges that were not dealt with last month. Always try to follow the original shape of the hedge and make sure that the base is slightly wider than the top, as this will make it less inclined to be badly damaged by heavy snow fall.

Cut back any pond or marginal plants that are starting to flop into the water; this is always a problem towards the end of the summer and into autumn, and by removing the leaves you will stop them rotting off or falling into the bottom of the pond where they later rot and produce toxic gasses.

ANTS

Ants can be a real menace for much of the summer. Their tunnelling activities can loosen the soil so much around plant roots that the plants end up suffering from drought, as their fine root hairs are no longer in close contact with the soil particles and moisture. But perhaps the habit they have which gardeners dislike even more is their biting. Ant bites can be quite painful, especially when sustained in large numbers!

Disturbing the nests using a garden fork, and then applying a proprietary ant killer, may solve the problem, but start by trying to control only those nests that are in parts of the garden where they are most irritating, as it is unlikely that you will kill them all off. There is also a biological control available and this can be used without risk to other wild or domesticated animals: if you happen to keep a few hens, or have a neighbour who does, it may be worth disturbing a nest and then inviting a hen round for a feast – mine certainly love them!

BLOSSOM-END ROT

Tomatoes may develop a black, leathery patch at the lower- or blossom-end of some of their fruits. This is known as blossom-end rot and is the result of a deficiency of calcium within the fruit. If the compost or soil is not constantly adequately moist, even if there is plenty of calcium in the compost, plant roots will not be able to take it up as conditions are too dry. This deficiency then causes cells at the blossom-end to collapse and blacken.

If the problem develops, remove the affected fruits (any ripe parts can be cooked up and eaten perfectly safely) and ensure that the plants are regularly watered and fed. This should allow later developing fruits to ripen normally. Tomatoes growing in small pots or growing bags are more likely to succumb to this problem than those growing in large containers or greenhouse borders, so next year see if you can find larger containers, as the larger volume of compost they contain is much easier to keep moist.

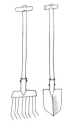

Although most frequently seen on tomatoes, occasionally sweet peppers will show the same symptoms.

Notes

September

Early September

ORNAMENTALS

Sow hardy annual flowers including nigella, cornflowers, candytuft, Shirley poppies, larkspur and clarkia now – these will be ready to flower next summer.

Planting can begin now for most bulbs, including daffodils and other narcissus, sciallas, crocus, snowdrops, miniature iris and muscari, to mention a few.

As soon as the weather starts to cool down, you can start to plant container-grown trees, shrubs and climbers, and know that they are likely to establish far better than if you'd done it a few months ago.

Make sure that autumn-flowering perennials, such as Japanese anemones, asters, Michaelmas daisies and sedums, are all well supported. These autumnal beauties may have put on a bit more growth than expected, especially if the weather has been warm and moist, and so may need a little extra support. Heavy rain or gusty winds might otherwise be their downfall.

Apply a sulphate of potash or rock potash feed to any containers that include herbaceous perennials. This will help to give them a little extra strength to survive the coming winter unscathed.

Start to plant out vegetables for overwintering. If you have sent off for these, get them planted as soon as they are delivered – take precautions against hungry pigeons as soon as the plants are in the ground by installing netting or net- or mesh-covered cages.

Lift any potatoes that are still in the ground. This should be the last of the main crop varieties and once they are out of the soil, leave them on the surface for a few hours so that the skin can dry off thoroughly. Store only undamaged and seemingly perfectly healthy tubers – any showing pest attack, or those that have been damaged on lifting, need to be eaten first. Store tubers in paper or hessian sacks in a dark, cool but frost-free place, such as a shed or garage.

Make further sowings of rocket and spinach as well as a little pak choi and you will benefit as, sown now, the resulting plants should not run to seed too quickly.

To avoid winter moth problems on next year's crop of apples, fix grease bands around the base of each tree trunk. Fixed properly, these sticky bands prevent the female winter moth from climbing up the trunk and, as she cannot fly, this means she cannot lays eggs from which the caterpillars would hatch.

Plant new strawberries before the middle of this month, so that their roots can put on a bit of growth whilst the soil is still fairly warm and moist.

Give yourself a good workout: aerate established lawns, especially those on heavy soils or those that are subjected to heavy wear and tear. For small areas, use a garden fork driven in to a depth of 10 cm or more, but for larger or severely compacted areas buy or hire a hollow tine aerator.

Continue to remove blanket weed from ponds – twining it around a bamboo cane works well. There is unlikely to be much more growth on it this year, so this is one job you will be able to give up for a few months!

Get planting – autumn is a great time to plant most things including trees, shrubs and climbers. If the weather is still quite warm, or there has been little rain, then wait until later in the month or in to October.

Create new lawns from seed sown now, but remember to keep them well watered if the weather is dry. Lawns can also be made from turf laid now. Use a suitable grass-seed mixture to overseed bare or sparse areas on existing lawns.

Use a spring-tined rake to scarify or aggressively rake the lawn to remove all the built-up dead grasses and debris (known as thatch). If your lawn contains a lot of moss, use a moss killer first if you haven't done this already, then wait the specified time on the packet before scarifying.

Late September

ORNAMENTALS

Continue to cut back deteriorating leaves on pond and marginal plants so that they do not flop in to the water and rot.

Plant up pots and bowls of bulbs for indoor displays in the house – the easiest to use are described as 'forced' or 'treated' by the grower/nursery, so that they will reliably flower at the stated time. Hyacinths and paperwhites always work very well.

Prune climbing roses that have finished flowering. Prune out dead, damaged, diseased or dying stems first, and prune old stems back to 8–10 cm above soil level. Prune back side shoots on the branches of the main framework of stems to about three buds, then tie the new stems into the support system.

Transplant biennials such as wallflowers and Sweet Williams now – move them into their flowering place, ideally in a sunny spot. If you have not raised your own you should be able to buy good plants from garden centres and pick-your-own outlets. I find bare-root wallflowers perform best.

Lift and divide clumps of overcrowded herbaceous perennials that have performed for the year. Discard the central weak parts of the clump and replant the outer, more vigorous sections into well-prepared soil.

Make sure any plants that you wish to keep but which are not completely hardy (many fuchsias, pelargoniums, ivy-leafed geraniums, for example) are brought back in to a suitable greenhouse, porch or frame.

Continue to plant spring-flowering bulbs.

Check stored potatoes every few weeks. Despite your efforts to bag up only those in perfect health, you need to check as one rotting tuber soon causes the problem to spread.

Plant onions from onion sets (mini onions) now. There should be a good selection available in garden centres, so choose a colour and intensity of flavour to suit your needs. Plant so that the thin wispy top of each set is just protruding above soil level, then cover the entire row with fleece or net to prevent birds pulling the sets out of the ground.

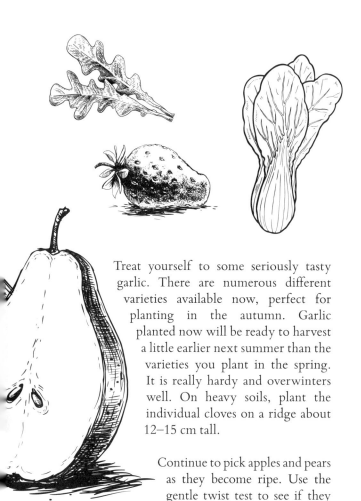

Treat yourself to some seriously tasty garlic. There are numerous different varieties available now, perfect for planting in the autumn. Garlic planted now will be ready to harvest a little earlier next summer than the varieties you plant in the spring. It is really hardy and overwinters well. On heavy soils, plant the individual cloves on a ridge about 12–15 cm tall.

Continue to pick apples and pears as they become ripe. Use the gentle twist test to see if they are ready to be harvested – cup the fruit in your hand, twist it and if it comes away, it's ready.

Keep all young overwintering vegetable plants well watered if the weather is dry; they need all the help they can get so that they establish before the winter arrives.

Continue to scarify the lawn; rake it vigorously to remove debris including thatch (dead grass) and dead moss that has accumulated now that the moss killer has taken effect.

Fix nets over ponds to catch autumn leaves – if allowed to rot in the pond they will produce gasses which could then prove toxic to fish during the winter months. I think a double net system works best: the first net can be firmly fixed in place, then lay a second one over the top. Empty out the top net as soon as it has fallen leaves on it and it will be easy to replace as you just lay it in place over the lower net.

Carefully lift any congested or over-vigorous pond and marginal plants out now, divide and cut them back as necessary – this is not a job you need to do every year, but leave it too long and things soon get out of hand!

Make yourself a leaf-mould bin so you can make full use of all those falling leaves. It is better to rot down leaves separately from your compost system, as they disintegrate at a slower pace. The easiest bin is more like a cage: take four 120-cm-tall posts and drive them into the ground, marking the corners of a square. Then, attach galvanised chicken wire all around the outside of the posts to create a cage you can fill with leaves as soon as they start to fall in earnest.

TIPS FOR *September*

Autumn is almost always the best time to get new ornamental plants into the ground; plants establish well now that the soil is getting moister, but is also retaining some of its summer warmth, so get planting!

Things to look for when buying plants:

Whenever possible, buy from a known source of good plants: a favourite local garden centre or nursery, or from a specialist nursery.

Avoid buying anything that does not look healthy; check plants over carefully for signs of pests and diseases.

Avoid plants potted in compost covered with algae, weeds or liverworts.

Big is rarely better – smaller plants generally establish and grow away better than those that have been on display for too long.

When buying bedding or herbaceous plants, avoid those which are in full flower; instead, choose sturdy plants with plenty of buds.

Most shrubs, trees and climbers establish best if planted in autumn (or failing this in spring) so this is the best time to buy them.

Checklist for successful planting:

Choose plants that suit the positions you have available – consider soil type (alkaline or acid, heavy or sandy), aspect (the direction the site faces and so the amount of sun the plant will receive), temperature, and the potential size of the plant once full-grown.

Prepare the site well first – remove debris and weeds, dig soil over to alleviate compaction, incorporate bulky organic matter such as compost to feed the soil and improve its texture.

Dig a good-sized planting hole and add extra planting compost, forking it in gently and adding some fertiliser too.

If the plant's rootball is at all dry, stand it in a bucket of water for a couple of hours before planting.

Gently but firmly tease out the rootball to encourage the roots to grow out in to their new surroundings.

Plant at the correct depth – unless otherwise stated on the plant label, ensure that the top of the compost covering the rootball is level with the soil surface.

Firm soil in well to prevent air pockets, and then ensure that the plant is kept well watered, especially during dry weather.

Notes

October

Early October

ORNAMENTALS

Continue to plant spring-flowering bulbs in flower beds and borders, as well as in pots and other containers. They are really good value and will bring delightful spring colour year after year. It may take a little time (and more than a little extra effort!), but try to plant them as deep as the pack suggests; they will do better, last longer and you will be less likely to dig them up by mistake when you are planting other flowers nearby.

Cut or pick off any semi-evergreen leaves that are showing signs of powdery mildew growth. Plants such as pulmonarias often retain many of their leaves over the winter, and this allows the mildew to persist. A timely clean-up now will not only reduce the disease problem next year but also keep the plants looking as attractive as possible over the coming winter.

Go on a slug and snail hunt – looking for the pests and clumps of their eggs in and around flower borders at this time of year often yields large numbers of these infuriating pests! See Tips for March on slug and snail removal.

Clear autumn leaves from flower beds as promptly as you can if the bed contains small plants, as these are easily swamped by the leaves and, as they deteriorate, the crowns of the plants may start to rot.

Make sure that vegetables are kept well weeded, so that competition is kept to a minimum – as temperatures fall, they need all the help they can get if they are to continue to establish and grow well.

Pick the last of the unripe tomatoes, as the plants are likely to deteriorate rapidly now. If the plants are still in good condition and free from fuzzy brownish-grey mould, you can afford to wait a week or two. Once off the plant, provided the fruits are in good condition, you can encourage them to ripen by placing several in a paper bag with an overripe banana. The banana gives off ethylene gas which speeds up ripening.

Sow a pot full of basil seed, lightly sprinkling it on the surface and covering with a millimetre or two of compost. Keep it in a propagator or on a warm windowsill with the compost just moist at all times. Basil is far too tender to be outside at this time of year, but makes a great windowsill herb.

If you get your skates on there is still time to plant some onion sets or autumn planting garlic, but hurry! As long as the bulbs you buy are free from mould and look and feel perfectly sound, with no signs of excessive softness or rot, they should still be fine.

Apply an autumn feed to your lawn, watering it in well if you choose a dry or granular form and especially if the weather is dry. As long as you select a fertiliser that is formulated specifically for autumn use, it will help to make up for the stresses of the summer past, and to strengthen the grass ready for the winter ahead.

Regularly rake fallen leaves off the lawn before they get rained on and become packed down into an impenetrable, immovable mass. Collect up all the leaves promptly, before the wind catches them and redistributes them again, and make them into leaf mould (see Late September General section for advice on how to make a leaf-mould bin).

In milder areas you can still safely sow grass seed or lay turf to make a new lawn, but for this to be successful at this late stage the soil must not be too wet or cold… so it is worth a risk but only if you are certain that there is a good chance the grass seed will germinate soon.

Continue with autumn lawn care, scarifying, aerating and removing weeds as suggested in September. However, if there has been heavy rain and the lawn is excessively wet, it would be best to wait for it to dry out a little or else you may do more damage than good.

Late October

ORNAMENTALS

Continue to plant as many spring-flowering bulbs as you can – in beds, borders, planters or even naturalised in grass beneath trees or large shrubs. If you can possibly spare the space then why not plant a few bulbs specifically for cutting. I have a small area of daffodils and other narcissus, iris, snowdrops and tulips, which are there just to allow a wonderful source of home-picked flowers for the house! Tulips are best planted this month, as this allows them to escape the dreaded 'tulip fire' infection.

Buy and plant some of the less common and very beautiful bulbs too such as *Camassias*, *Eremurus* and *Gladiolus communis* for flowering next summer. Follow the pack instructions carefully for best situation and planting depth, then cover the newly planted area with mesh to prevent the bulbs being dug up by squirrels, badgers and other local wildlife.

Have another collecting-up session, combing the grass or soil beneath shrubs and herbaceous perennials to remove fallen leaves that are harbouring disease. Provided you have a decent composting system, these leaves can safely be composted, or else you can incorporate them with the green-waste-collection material.

If peaches or nectarines were infected with the peach leaf curl fungus (puckered red and purple leaves which fall prematurely) earlier this year then it is essential that you rake up any infected leaves beneath or close to the tree. Many gardeners also swear by the use of a copper-based spray applied now, as the leaves are falling, as this helps to clean up the tree and reduce the problem next year.

Strawberry plants benefit from a seriously good tidy up at this time of year. Pick off all discoloured leaves (especially those showing reddish-purple leaf spotting) and add them to the compost heap. You should also remove any remaining runners from the plants as this will ensure that the main plant can retain its vigour, and hopefully crop better as a result.

Clear away the last of the tomatoes, sweet and chilli peppers and aubergines from greenhouses and frames, as soon as they have finished cropping. Provided the plants appear perfectly healthy (with maybe just a little grey mould!) they can safely be added to the compost bin or heap.

If you enjoy a little fresh parsley or mint with your meals it is definitely worth digging up a section from an established clump or plant. Just pot it on into a good-sized, well-drained container with some fresh compost and keep it on a well-lit windowsill where it should then be able to be useful for the next few months.

Continue to collect up fallen leaves from the nets on ponds and from the lawn. It may seem as if this is a never-ending job, and I have to confess to feeling the same, but it will be (mostly) over soon, and just think of all that lovely leaf mould you can make!

If collecting them from grassed areas is just too time consuming and you have a mower with a collection hopper or bag for the clippings, you can always mow the lawn and cut up and collect up the leaves at the same time. This works especially well if you are mowing up tougher leaves such as horse chestnut or sycamore, which then rot down much faster than usual because they have been minced up.

If you want to make use of leaves by rotting them down into leaf mould, but don't have enough space for a leaf mould bin, then why not make some in bin bags? Just cram the leaves into black bin liners, add a litre or two of water, fold the top of the bag over and hold it in place with a brick, then use a fork to puncture a few rows of holes in the bag. Stacked in an out-of-the-way spot (yes, they are not exactly attractive!) for 6–12 months they will then be full of lovely leaf mould.

Take every opportunity to plant this month – trees, shrubs, climbers and herbaceous plants should all establish well whilst the soil is moist and still fairly warm.

TOADSTOOLS IN LAWNS

This is the season for toadstools and there is one place you really don't want to see them, and that is covering your lawn. Start by trying to brush them off using a broom – if you do this regularly and promptly so that the caps have not had time to open (and so have not been able to spread spores) the problem may be solved.

However, if they keep on and on returning, despite your best efforts, then the toadstools are probably feeding not just on general debris beneath the lawn but on dead tree roots: this explains why they are growing in strangely straight lines. If this is the case, then the only good way to get rid of them is to excavate the dead roots on which they are feeding. Carefully cut the turf in the infested area, remove the offending root, fill the gap left with some good quality top soil, firm well and then replace the turf. At this time of year the grass should soon recover… and be toadstool free!

HONEY FUNGUS

Honey fungus (also known as Armillaria) is probably the problem that most gardeners fear most. With aggressive forms having the potential to kill most trees, shrubs, climbers and even some woodier herbaceous perennials, it is no wonder. At this time of year you may spot the toadstools – a gingery-brown mushroom shape, often (but not always) growing in clumps and associated with plants that are looking sickly. The toadstools have brown speckles on the tops of their caps and produce white spores. The toadstools themselves are not responsible for spreading the infection, but may confirm your suspicions or act as a warning. Infected plants have a creamy-white mushroom-smelling fungal sheet (the mycelium) sandwiched beneath the bark at the base of the trunk/main stem and/or beneath the bark on larger roots. It is this part which does the damage.

Infected plants should be removed, ideally together with their entire root system, as soon as possible. When you dig up the plant you may also find blackish, toughened fungal threads (commonly known as rhizomorphs or bootlaces), which should be removed as well.

When replanting, refer to a plant pests and diseases book for a full list of those plants that are more resistant to honey fungus, and those best to avoid.

Notes

November

Early November

ORNAMENTALS

If you grow tender plants, such as plumbago, passion flower, oleander or brugmansia (datura), in a conservatory or greenhouse, these can all be given a bit of a tidy-up by pruning them now. As you do this, also check the plants over for any overwintering pests and treat as necessary.

Continue to plant tulip bulbs. With their fantastically bright, showy colours they can brighten up even the dullest spring. Add them to existing containers and planters, window boxes and tubs, as well as using them in open ground. For best results choose as sunny and well-drained a spot as you can.

Protect the less hardy bulbs, such as nerines and agapanthus, especially if your garden is quite cold or exposed. Mounding some chunky woodchip over their crowns is generally enough to provide all the insulation needed.

Thin out the canes on established bamboos. Given a bit more space, the remaining canes will not only develop more quickly, but you will find that they move about more freely as well – one of the charms of a clump of bamboo! You can use those you remove as plant supports in the same way you would those you buy from a garden centre.

Make sure that all herb pots are either plunged into the soil in a sheltered spot in the garden or are well insulated to protect the roots against excessive cold. Also, check that the drainage holes have not become obscured as this can lead to (potentially fatal) waterlogging. Now is another good time to place pots on special 'pot feet' available from garden centres and pot suppliers – or, on larger planters, use bricks hidden beneath the pot to achieve the same effect. Raising a planter or pot above the surface helps to dramatically reduce the risk of the drainage holes becoming blocked.

Prune redcurrant, gooseberry and blackcurrant bushes if you have not already done so, aiming to keep the centres of the bushes 'open' and uncongested so that air can circulate well and

sunshine can reach the stems too. This should help to ensure that they fruit well and also helps to fend off disease problems.

As soon as fruit trees and bushes are dormant, they can be planted as bare-root specimens. These are generally available from specialist fruit nurseries and mail-order suppliers. The great thing about buying your fruit from these places is that they generally have by far the best selection of varieties, and the plants themselves tend to establish extremely well.

In very mild areas and in good years, if the weather is neither too wet nor too cold, there is still time to turf or, in mild areas, even sow grass seed. However, as this could be a risky pastime, ideally do so only for small areas and for repairing otherwise established lawns.

Check that rabbit guards are replaced or refitted around the base of trees and shrubs in areas where rabbits can be a problem. With their well-sharpened teeth these pests can devastate plants by removing bark and even ringing an entire tree.

Remove electrical pond pumps from ponds and water features now. Carefully dry them off, lightly grease metal parts and store them dry for the winter. Doing this reduces the risk of damage in very cold weather and also makes it less likely that they will get too clogged up with dead algae and other water debris.

If the weather has been wet, try to avoid walking on the lawn as damp turf treated in this way soon becomes compacted and then fails to thrive.

Brush toadstools off the lawn as soon as they appear (see Tips for October) but remember that the majority of toadstools that you find in the garden pose no threat to garden plants and indeed some may be beneficial.

Late November

ORNAMENTALS

Lift a few plants from established clumps of lily-of-the-valley, pot them up in a mixture of garden soil and loam-based compost and keep them in the greenhouse. Keep the roots only very slightly moist and then, given this extra bit of warmth and TLC, they will be ready to flower inside in mid spring.

Some ornamental grasses retain their good looks over the winter months, looking especially glamorous when covered with a spiky hoar frost. But others simply look awful and past their best, so you can cut these miserable ones back to 8–10 cm above the crown, taking care not to cut too closely and cause any damage to next year's potential.

Send off for a really good selection of seed, young plant and bulb catalogues, and peruse websites to see what is available for growing next year – this is a brilliant bad-weather activity, but take your time choosing or else you may find you order far more than you need (or can afford!). I always try to leave a 'cooling-off period' between deciding what I think I want and actually placing the order!

Spring-flowering bulbs are often dramatically reduced in price at this time of year, as garden centres fill their shelves with all things Christmassy. As long as bulbs appear good and show no sign of mould growth or softening they are still definitely worth buying – most years I plant some of them far later than this, and although the first year's flowering is often delayed somewhat, the results are almost always as good as with earlier plantings, and they do represent a brilliant bargain.

Start to prune apple and pear trees as soon as it is apparent that the trees are dormant. It is worth consulting a specialist fruit book for full details about the pruning methods and needs for each type of fruit and the form in which you are growing it – then, sharpen your secateurs and get started. If, however, you are pressed for time, the weather is too miserable for all that standing about, or you are not sure if the trees are fully dormant quite yet, you can wait as this is just the start of the fruit-tree pruning season.

Once tomatoes or other crops grown in planters, pots and growing bags have finished cropping they really should be composted or binned, but you can re-use the compost. I sometimes use it as soil mulch or fork it in to areas of the garden not used for vegetable gardening.

Or, if you have a suitable greenhouse, why not be even greener and before you do this, re-use it for sowing some winter lettuce?

Check that trained fruit trees are really well secured to their supports before they have to put up with the worst of the winter weather and being buffeted about in gales.

Keep nets or cages and mesh in place over overwintering brassicas as pigeons and other pests such as rabbits are likely to be getting hungrier now as their natural food sources start to become scarcer.

If you are sure that you will not be using items of garden furniture over the winter, clean them off and either put them under cover or cover them up so that they are protected from the worst of the winter weather.

Continue to order bare root trees, shrubs and hedging plants for planting later this month or during suitable weather this winter, i.e. when the soil is neither excessively wet nor frozen solid. Despite the way they often look when delivered, provided you keep up with the aftercare, bare-root plants generally establish extremely well and are very good value.

Check that arches and arbours, trellis and fencing are all in good order and well secured before winter gets a full grip. All these structures may have taken a battering in the autumn weather, which is often very windy, and now that there is less to do in the garden itself an hour or two spent doing some structural DIY could save you a lot of time later on.

Feed wild birds with suitable food and make sure that there is always a selection of quality snacks available for them, plus a source of clean water for drinking and bathing.

CORAL SPOT

As deciduous stems are now pretty well devoid of leaves, this is a good time to see the sort of things you wish were not there! Bright orange raised spots or pustules of coral spot are one of the easiest diseases to spot at this time of year. Coral spot is especially common on *Acer* species (maples) *Elaeagnus*, figs and magnolias. Although the fungus often attacks dead stems, it can also be quite aggressive and cause damage to living stems. If you see coral spot, use sharp secateurs or a saw to prune out the infected stem, cutting back into totally healthy wood and then binning or burning any infected material.

Coral spot may not be as nasty as some plant infections, but it can still cause quite a bit of dieback so it is definitely not something that you should leave lying around the garden, or put through a chipper to create chippings for paths, etc. If you can, always remove dead stems from trees and shrubs before you even see signs of coral spot fungus – by doing this you will help to prevent it spreading.

APPLE AND PEAR CANKER

Apples and pears can both be attacked by the same fungal canker. Infected stems show slightly raised, flaky patches of bark and these cankers may spread around the entire stem, branch or even the main trunk and ring it, causing the growth past that point to deteriorate and die off. If the main trunk is attacked then the whole tree may be killed. Most apples and pears, including ornamental varieties, may be damaged by this canker, but any tree that is not growing vigorously will be all the more susceptible.

At this time of year it is very easy to spot cankered stem as the branches are leafless. Any cankered stems should be pruned out as part of the winter pruning regime and then they must be binned or burned as apple and pear canker is very contagious (see Tips for February). If a larger limb or the main trunk is infected then it may be possible to save it, provided you catch the infection early and then carefully pare away all the cankered parts, right back to perfectly healthy wood.

Notes

December

Early December

ORNAMENTALS

Plant tulips – these are often available in garden centres now at knock-down prices. Provided the soil is not very wet or cold, you can also get away with planting daffodils this late – just expect a show of flowers a few weeks later than your neighbours! If the soil is very cold or wet the best place to plant any bulbs is in good-sized planters.

Provide protection for the less hardy or exotic plants that have become so popular in recent years. Tree ferns, palms, 'hardy' bananas, cordylines and giant rhubarb need to be protected from winter wet and cold, especially in cooler parts of the country or if particularly cold or wet weather is forecast. Multiple layers of fleece or other materials that allow at least a degree of air circulation work well for the top growth, but avoid polythene and bubble wrap as this soon encourages dampness and, subsequently, rotting.

Plant up some containers for winter colour – use the wide selection of lovely winter interest plants that are available from garden centres and nurseries and even many markets at this time of year, and under-plant with some miniature spring-flowering bulbs.

If the soil is not really wet (and so prone to becoming compacted), start preparing the soil in areas that you wish to use for vegetable growing next year. On heavier soils a garden fork works better than a spade as it will help to aerate rather than compact or smear the soil.

Manuring a vegetable plot really helps to increase productivity and now, while the beds are relatively empty, you can really get going in earnest. Check that any manure you buy in is well rotted, free from unwanted debris such as baler twine and plastics, and if possible check that the animals from which it originated have not been grazing on herbicide-contaminated land.

Take a few minutes to check stakes and ties that help to support your fruit trees, bushes and canes are in good condition and firmly in place, yet not causing any restriction around the plants' stems.

Provided that the soil is neither excessively wet nor frozen, this is a good time to plant new fruit trees and bushes. There is still plenty of time to do this however, so if you don't have the plants to hand yet don't rush out and buy the first thing you see, but spend some time researching what works well in your locality and try to find a specialist fruit nursery in the vicinity.

Keep a watch on the weather forecast and make sure that you lag outdoor taps before there is any chance of them freezing. This really is a job that should be done sooner rather than later, and before there is any chance of damage being done. You can buy special pipe insulation materials at DIY stores, or create your own using multiple layers of bubble-wrap polythene topped with some old carpet. Outdoor pipes that rupture can cause serious damage and water wastage, so, if possible, isolate them from the mains.

If you are growing pots of forced bulbs for indoor colour, check the pots and bowls regularly and bring them into a cool but well-lit room once shoots are about 3 cm tall. After a week or two they can then be moved into a warmer room as their buds or flower spikes start to fatten and colour up.

This is still a good time to plant new hedges as bare-root transplants and seedlings of some great hedging plants are available by mail order, and are brilliant value. (See Tips for December).

Try to prevent ponds and garden water features from icing up. The old idea of floating a football, or perhaps a plastic water bottle on the surface of the water really does help – the movement it creates reduces the likelihood of freezing, and if the surface does freeze some of the pressure this would exert on the sides of the pond is reduced, as it is absorbed by the ball or plastic bottle.

Late December

ORNAMENTALS

Place orders for seeds if you have not already done so – the best selection is often available from websites and catalogues and by ordering promptly, you are more likely to get what you want.

Make sure that the last of the plant supports and stakes from beds and borders are collected up; if you clean off soil and allow them to dry, provided they are stored in a dry shed or garage, they should still be in good condition to re-use next year.

Use your foot to re-firm the soil around the base of any trees, shrubs or climbers planted within the last few months. Windy conditions earlier on can loosen even the best-planted specimen.

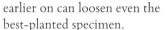

Bring a few stems of holly that still have berries into a cool shed or garage, so that you can use it for seasonal decoration. Do this now and there is a far greater chance of you getting to some before the birds have eaten them all.

On windy sites, reduce the length of any very tall rose stems using sharp secateurs. This will minimise the risk of the plants being damaged or loosened in the soil in any windier weather that is yet to come.

Leave snowfall on flower beds as it will help to insulate more tender plants from some of the colder temperatures that are likely to follow in the next few months.

Winter pruning of fruit trees is important, especially if you are growing your fruit in trained forms such as espaliers, fans, and step-overs. Start or continue with this job as the weather conditions dictate – if it is quite mild I would get on and do it, but if you are having bitterly cold weather then you can delay a little longer in hope of less finger-numbing conditions! As you prune look out for signs of apple canker (see Tips for November) and deal with this promptly.

If you own a heated propagator or somewhere to grow small plants on in the warm, sow a few winter lettuces and radish, and perhaps some rocket. These will grow much more slowly at this time of year but will still add a little lovely home-grown interest to your meals.

Continue to plant fruit trees, bushes and canes as weather conditions allow. There are lots of wonderful varieties available, especially if you go to a specialist nursery. If you have fruit plants delivered and the soil is frozen solid or otherwise unworkable you can safely store the plants with some moist compost around their roots for a week or so – make sure that they are kept somewhere that is cold, but that the roots are protected from frosts or freezing.

If you haven't got a heated propagator either treat yourself to one or ask for it as a seasonal gift. The range of plants you can raise from seed will be massively increased by this fantastic piece of kit: vegetables, herbs, annuals, perennials and maybe some exotics too!

Buy in a stock of good-quality seeds and cuttings compost for seed sowing – this is often on special offer at this time of year. Choose bags that are undamaged and not excessively compacted; put at least one bag in your greenhouse to warm it up slightly ready for the first lot of seed sowing.

Remember that freezing weather can make paths, steps and driveways dangerously slippery and applying salt or grit can really improve the situation (see General section in Early February), but if you apply these materials ensure that nearby flower beds, hedges or large plants are not contaminated – use sparingly!

Treat yourself to a few day trips or even just a few hours one weekend and visit some large gardens for ideas – you'll be amazed at just how many great plants are available at this time of year. I always keep a special look out for plants with delicious winter perfume too (such as witch-hazels and daphnes). Take a notebook and pencil with you, as it is always harder to remember tricky plant and variety names than you imagine it will be!

BARE-ROOT HEDGING PLANTS

If you are contemplating planting a new hedge this, the dormant season, is perfect and many plants are available right now as bare-root specimens, ideal for the job and good value. Most need to be planted at approximately 45 cm spacing – for a really lovely dense hedge, plant in two parallel, staggered rows, with about 45 cm between the rows. Make sure that the soil is improved with some well-rotted manure or planting compost if you want to make initial maintenance easier and increase the rate at which the plants grow. Most importantly, protect new hedges against the ravages of creatures such as rabbits and deer, both of which can devastate a hedge, especially when it is so very new.

There are many good-value hedging plants available by mail order and from websites including:

Beech (*Fagus sylvatica*, green and/or copper)

Blackthorn (*Prunus spinosa*)

Field maple (*Acer campestre*)

Guelder rose (*Viburnum opulus*)

Hawthorn (*Crataegus monogyna*)

Hornbeam (*Carpinus*)

Privet (*Ligustrum*)

Wild roses (e.g. *Rosa canina, Rosa rugosa*)

Yew (*Taxus baccata*)

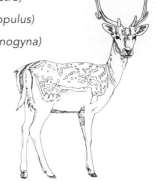

WINTER CONTAINERS

It is so easy to brighten up a terrace, patio or balcony or even the front steps if you plant up some containers full of winter colour. Choose containers that have plenty of good drainage holes and that are as large as possible, as the compost within them is less likely to become frozen in harsh winter weather. I like to line containers with bubble-wrap polythene, taking care not to block the drainage holes in the process, and this really helps to keep the plant roots insulated against damage. Select good-quality multi-purpose compost and some bright cheery colours to lift your spirits in the cold, gloomy weather ahead! Some of my favourites include: hellebores, winter-flowering cyclamen, early narcissus and crocus, cineraria 'Silver Dust', winter-flowering pansies, winter pom-pom daisies, snowdrops, winter-flowering heathers and variegated ivies.

Have a great gardening year, and I hope you enjoy all your garden has to offer!

Notes

Image credits